I SPY

At the LIBRARY

by Spencer Brinker

Consultant:
Beth Gambro
Reading Specialist
Yorkville, Illinois

Contents

BEARPORT
PUBLISHING

New York, New York

At the Library

Where am I?
I am at the library!

What do I spy?

I spy a shelf.

It is big.

I spy a chair.

It is red.

I spy a table.

It is round.

I spy a lamp.

It is green and gold.

I spy a computer.

It is black.

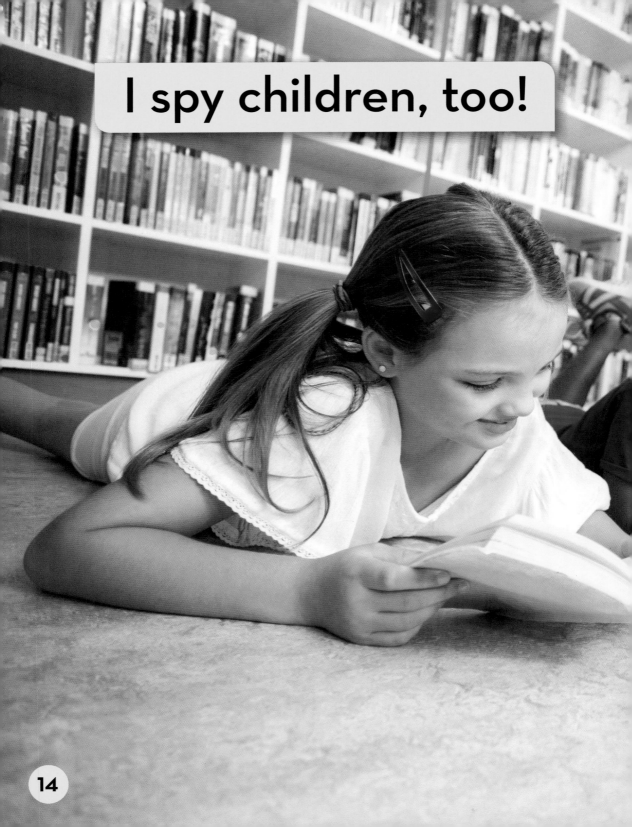

I spy children, too!

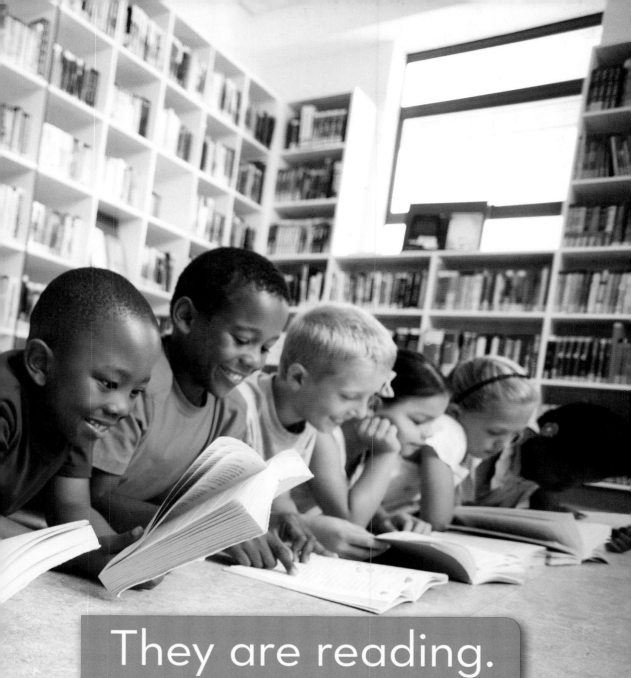

They are reading.
Shhh!

Key Words

chair

computer

lamp

shelf

table

Index

About the Author

Spencer Brinker lives and works in New York City. In such a big city, you can spy almost anything.

Teaching Tips

Before Reading

✔ Guide readers on a "picture walk" through the text by asking them to name the things shown.

✔ Discuss book structure by showing children where text will appear consistently on pages.

✔ Highlight the supportive pattern of the book. Note the consistent number of sentences and words found on each alternating page.

During Reading

✔ Encourage readers to "read with your finger" and point to each word as it is read. Stop periodically to ask children to point to a specific word in the text.

✔ Reading strategies: When encountering unknown words, prompt readers with encouraging cues such as:

- **Does that word look like a word you already know?**

- **It could be _____ , but look at _____ . What words make sense here?**

- **Check the picture.**

After Reading

✔ Write the key words on index cards.

- **Have readers match them to pictures in the book.**

- **Have children sort words by category (words that are five letters long, for example).**

✔ Ask readers to identify their favorite page in the book. Have them read that page aloud.

✔ Ask children to write their own sentences. Encourage them to use the same pattern found in the book as a model for their writing.

Credits: Cover, © studiocasper/iStock and © g215/Shutterstock; 2–3, © Chungking/Deposit Photos; 4–5, © connel/Shutterstock; 6–7, © pornpan jayanama/Shutterstock; 8–9, © Kaypendragon/Shutterstock; 10–11, © Adkasai/iStock and © Indypendenz/Shutterstock; 12–13, © Gan Hui/Dreamstime; 14–15, © Wavebreakmedia Ltd/Dreamstime; 16T (L to R), © pornpan jayanama/Shutterstock and © Gan Hui/Dreamstime; 16B (L to R), © Adkasai/iStock, © Indypendenz/Shutterstock, © connel/Shutterstock, and © Kaypendragon/Shutterstock.

Publisher: Kenn Goin   **Senior Editor:** Joyce Tavolacci   **Creative Director:** Spencer Brinker   **Photo Researcher:** Thomas Persano

Library of Congress Cataloging-in-Publication Data in process at time of publication (2019)
Library of Congress Control Number: xxxxx
ISBN-13: 978-1-64280-222-1 (library binding) | ISBN-13: 978-1-64280-395-2 (paperback)

10 9 8 7 6 5 4 3 2 1